CHERISH WHAT YOU HAVE NOT TO LOSE IT

YOU MIGHT NOT UNDERSTAND BETTER OF WHAT YOU HAVE NOT UNTIL YOU PUT THEM INTO FULL UTILIZATION

ADETOPE ADENIJI

<u>DEDICATION</u>

The book is dedicated to the Almighty God, the source of all things and the maker of all inspirational conceptions who approves and disapproves all imaginative and exhibiting values. To Him all glory, honour and majesty belong to.

And also, to those who have thought me on how to handle all situations with calmness and to be contended with all circumstances, to make out a reasonable outcome, and to have in my thinking things that can contribute to the existence positively at all cost.

Table of contents

ACKNOWLEDGMENT

My sincere appreciation goes to my family members, wife, child, relatives, friends and all the lovers of our books, services and musical initiative. To the schools I attended and the churches where the wisdom of God had been given. The box of my wisdom. The Very Rev'd and Mrs. J.A. Adeniji(rtd), Sir and Rev. Mrs A.B. Aladekomo, Baba and Mama Ayo Oni, The Very Rev'd(Prof) and Mrs Ayo Richards and hosts of the ministers in the sanctuary of God, all the teachers of all sorts of reasonable studies, men of humanitarian concern and other individuals of thought and values of the reasonable thought as catalyst to the growth and development of the world. I say thank you for the insight and your dearest support.

To my siblings, Bro Dapo, Segun, Wemimo, Oyinade and Florence, you are so precious to me. My friends that are uncountable in number in which thousands of the readers are part of, I quite appreciate you and your assistance. Mr Oyewo Joseph, who proof read the book, you are highly appreciated.

The church I attend at the moment, Wesley Chapel and every other Methodist

Churches, and all the churches in theworld, thank you all for the installation of the faith and godliness.

The schools I have attended, my teachers and colleague have impacted me exceedingly, lots of appreciation.

God bless you all.

INTRODUCTION

Everybody knows not what they possess at a point in time in life till they realize either by a sudden subconscious ness or by another individual sharing such a gift and trait with them. Whatever you have that are not noted on time, or that do not give an added advantage to your status in life is a waste.

Fortunately every individual has within him all what it takes them to flourish in life, but quite unfortunate that most of us do not know what we have. This however leads to the problem or the other that we often count to be misfortune in our ideology or conclusion.

When a man possesses hundred lots of grains of maize in his hand, and he never attempted to plant them, there can never be a magic to reap a set of corn, or to have a harvest of thousand folds of what he has with him. What I am saying invariably is that, there is virtually nothing you have with you or in you that cannot be planted even if they seem dead. The dead plants in a man are the thought considered impossible.

A man must be extremely fast and trained to understand the exact place at which what he has can be put to use to make a

better living. If what you know most is interacting with the people around, it must be jealously guided and be put at its best to make you and to create you a relevant avenue to excel.

The funniest aspect of life is however that, if you fail to determine what you have or someone other than you fails to mention it to you to be able to make the very best use of it, that which you have and which is yours will be expended on another person's purpose to climb to the stage of honour. Pathetically, one might not realize on time of the worth been expended on another person's obligation and by the time you regain or recover yourself, what you have would have been

turned to terror to be used due to the economic implication and value someone else had given to it. By then, you can only see the worth value of what you have been converted to, but the sequence of the process entails or the channels to understand yourself properly at a point you observed yourself will set the intimidation of not going back or thinking of being self-reliance.

However, this book is to encourage every reader on how to cherish what they have, to make the best use of them to become who they are meant to be, and not only that, but to have their specific guide and contribution to the environment at which they live.

Sincerely, not everyone will set a legacy with what he has, but as many that are willing to have an impact should be encouraged, most especially at the tender age to be discovered.

Tope Adeniji

CHAPTER ONE (1)

UNDERSTANDING WHAT YOU HAVE

When you are looking at understanding something thing, it means that such a thing must have been well tested and not only that, but you must know the way it operates to bring the expected result. When a man understands a particular issue, he knows better the purpose and the necessity to make it work for him. Understanding is based on different testing both within one's immediate environment and in the world. Though not at all times what you have to do can be tested prior to making them manifested at the physical realm, but it is a must to be well natured and examine them at the realm higher than the physical before their application.

To understand what you have means that
you must know and be ascertained that
what you have can work for you. The
result of what you have to do starts right
away from you. Without having trust and
better knowledge on what you do,
someone's interference may cause you to
neglect or abandon the project out
rightly.

When you understand what you have,
you will know the need to have it in place
and to give the very best zeal and passion
to make it happen. What makes people
most at times reluctant of acting on a
specific duty or obligation is never their
inability not to carry such duty out but
their inability to realize the essence of

doing what they have to do.

It is when one understands his purpose and what to do that he can swerve or digress with the multiplicity of inbuilt skills and talent. This is when you realize the variations of tactical approaches that should be employed to make the end of a project a realization. It is a time at which you foresee the huddles and impediments and get set for an alternative way or solution.

Looking at the academic region, suppose that some of the students were picked for an examination and the manuscripts or hand out on which they will be tested were made available and given to them, each of them will study the book to their tastes and not only that, in case of general study or lecture, the way at which each of the student digest the topic in question is different from a person to other. However, the testing field, which is the examination will avail to each student the opportunity to experiment their level of understand ability of the topic. The conviction and the degree of being able to deduce all what the topic relates on makes the different measure of performances and the result of each of them.

What I am saying is that, the level of understanding you have as regards what you have, brings a better degree of having a standard clue on what you are going through in life. This is what makes you to know that a stumbling stone can be converted to a machine gun to accomplish your desire in life.

The more the level of understanding of what you stand to gain as regards your commitment, the better are the chances you stand to have to fulfill the intention. This is however the reason why a man of a particular view must earnestly have a private brain storm towards his ambition and purpose to be fulfilled.

There are several things that are however very essential to be considered, if truly a man understands his mission in life to be able to effect them accordingly, else, it will be a thing of dream without a fulfillment. These are however:

(a)   **The time at which what you have should manifest;** there must be a time for everything in life, such is time of birth and death, time to move and to stop, time to talk and to make it an action, time to think and time to effect the thought, time to play and time to be serious, time to offer selfless services and time to look at the economic benefit of what you do, time to study and time to teach and several others which are quite essential to meet up with the standard expected of a man to be substantially made.

(b)   **How to make it to work:** here, I am trying to say that, no matter how good or bad your intention in life looks like, without it working or being experimented, you can never have them. There is need to make your values and ability working and not ordinarily working, but to work in correlation with your mission and vision. If your faith is greater than that of any other human, and all what you can perceive are not experimented, your faith will without argument be void and disused. Faith without work amounts to vanity. Therefore, the need to make what you have to work; to have the expected end of the pre-thought.

(c)   The return on it must be cleared to you; this means that, you must be able to think of what the result of the conclusive decision looks like. There must be a certain purpose of the cause of any action taken by you, you must be able to identify the time at which you are growing and the time at which you are coming down in line of the operation stated. Hence you must be well-cleared of the evaluation of your intention to meet up with the expected standard of your purpose.

(d)   The environment at which your value is required must be analyzed; not all the environment is good for your objective and intention. There must be a thorough study of the place at which your dream can germinate not to have it at a wrong place. There is every tendency of all the grains of maize to grow. But the determination of their germination is in line with the various places of their planting. One should not expect a grain that falls on the fertile land to produce as that on the rock, it is impossible. There is definitely a place at which you are extremely needed, where your value is more expedient, and not until such a place is arrived at, all what you have might be for your use all alone without any tangible effect in the world you live in.

(e)   Its season of operation must be identified; here, what I meant by the phrase is that, there are many obligation that go well in all seasons, whereas, many have a specific season for their needs.

Take for an instance, in the music world, the Christmas songs are not needed in the Easter period and so forth. The period of need of what you need to do must be well noted to fashion your contribution in line with the prevailing desire and wants to achieve your pre-tangential motives.

(f)   The set of people to make use of your products and services must be identified. This means that you can not just move around to meet with the set of individuals that are not in need of your value, and think you can excel or have an edge way. The set of individuals that are meant to use your product and services must be clearly figured out to be able to have a penetration into the term success, hence, the effort and struggling will only be futile and irrelevant.

(g)   The difficulties in association with the task must be noted; in any form of task in life to be carried out, there will always be challenges and difficulties. It is however of very great importance to be able to envisage the highest point of difficulty that can emanate and be well prepared to manage them whenever they are encountered. Having the preparedness to resolve issues of any kind when they are noticed is the encouraging factor to never be depressed when the storm of life arises.

There are many other things which must be of concern to have your best working out for your purpose, for the world at large to be in the light of it, to be able to pave way for your differentiated view and idea to be noted and have the necessary regards from all the phases of group of individuals and organization, else, the value you have will be completely stolen and drifted from you, and the most painful part of it is that, not that it will be completely taken away from you, but you will be made inactive to have dominion on them, which means, you will still be at work, giving what you have, but in control of another man for his own developmental purpose and economic benefit.

Therefore, understanding what a man has is quite very important and essential to have a mission accomplished, and to get the maximum control of the talents, traits and value.

CHAPTER TWO (2)

IDENTIFICATION OF YOUR POTENTIAL

The composition of a man is never what a man can quickly get to know within a short period of time, but it takes processes and series of stages to know it. The point remains that, there is no one created without a specific identified quality or character that is not synonymous to him and that is the reason why someone's strange attitude amazes another man most at times.

When looking at the identification of a particular object or a certain issue, there is need to know such a particular thing or object before it can be appropriately identified. Identification is quite different from understanding what you have. It is

very possible you can identify your potential but yet unable to understand it.

While thinking of identification, I meant that a man should be able to analyze and to state or recognize things that are synonymous to his capacity and ability. This is when one can strictly say that, I can do a certain thing or the other or knowing within him secretly of what his composition looks like.

In the book do not be hindered by the limitation around you, you will deduce that I said that the true worth and value of man is never measureable: which means that each a man has all what it takes to be who he is meant to be. What someone cannot do, is what another man can do, which simply says that our component are immensurable in nature.

Also, I was trying to portray the process in discovery oneself, if I am not oblivious, I said you can easily discover yourself in each a day's transaction you commit yourself to, and also, you may get to know yourself through the reaction of the people on what you are doing. This can simply be examined in the eulogy, encomium, praise and honour or the rejection, abandonment and complaint in your action towards the fulfilling of a set project.

If a man cannot fulfill the aspect of
identification of what he possesses, there
might not be need for him to cherish what
he has, this is as a result of the dis-
connectivity between what he has, how
to identify it and having the feeling to
cherish it. What I am trying to buttress is
that, you must at all cost find and get to
know that you have something before you
can think of the due honour to be given to
it, which means that, what you do not
know that you have can never be
jealously cherished and guided.

A man may not be able to fight for what
he cannot identify; else, he will fight
blindly. You as an individual can only fight
for your right or your possession when
you can identify what exactly you are

aiming at, not what you do not know or cannot identify as a person. Identification of your mission and purpose is what compels you to stage a determination of having it or lose something worthwhile to regain it.

As a growing up individuals or an adult, one must be able to identify his aspect of the best chance of ascending to his projected viewed destination, or else, he will be where he has no mind to be, which most at times leads to no-where. It is better to move into the identified aspect of one's life other than being a copycat that tend to venture into a particular decision and obligation as a result of seeing that many blossom while having it.

Very necessary for the parent and guidance to have a thorough study of the upcoming generation to identify the aspect in which they are versatile and try to be a guide till they are actualized. Compelling the children or the growing ones on a particular discipline or work might be a reduction on the performance level of a child or exterminate his or her interest to be who exactly he is supposed to be in life.

However, as it was pointed out beforehand, there are thousands of potentials in each man and all these potentials can seriously be put into use to achieve their goals, but that which you are pleased with and which cost you less of ambiguity to accomplish should be the ultimate aim to be made, else, one might continuously exert his ability on the fruitless effort which finally ends in futility.

The identification of one's potential and composition is quite necessary and relevant to be made, and not only to be made, but to be able to cherish what he has and guide it jealously to get fulfilled.

CHAPTER THREE (3)

ALERTNESS TO MAKE AN IMPACT

There is no amount of the level of your capability or ability that can make any meaningful impact if they are not made into action. Many have very good ideas and purpose that should have led them to the apex level of places in life but yet, they are in one way or the other afraid of practicing what they have conceived or procrastinating on the effectiveness of their dream.

You as a person must be conscious of the need to dramatize what you have. I have several friends, both old and young while I was trying to learn an instrument or the other with the great urge and the passion to learn such instrument, but most at times, they forget that anything that is practical in life is practical and must take part of the available resources that men are surrounded with before they can be turned to reality, and sincerely, nothing comes into existence base on doing nothing on its manifestation.

Without the readiness and preparedness to make an impact in life, you might be there at a particular time, in a place unknown, whereas you are to be somewhere else. Alertness to make an impact is the self-motivation or drive to roll and conform with the presence while viewing and projecting for the futuristic changes and transformation that might not have come in place but definitely without a doubt takes place when someone is set to have it.

A man must be fully set enough to hit his target at the point at which it is needed to be reacted to, and to move when there is need to move to be able to accomplish his motive. I was trying to address the issue of timing while looking at the first chapter, I said that, for each a program and action, there must be time, and the time must never be made to be wasted or unused to arrive at the projected evidence or proof of mans' intention.

As the world revolves, there are thousands of gaps that are at all times opened to be filled and occupied. In such position and gap are where the contributions of men are essential to fill up. When men could not meet up with the movement of how the world revolves, they are made useless or irrelevant. This however leads to the depression that man encounter to either catch up with another opportunity or not. I am of the stand that, in each movement of time and period, there are thousands of opportunity man can tap into, and there are many avenues to be made, but man tends to be paralyzed and distorted in their ambition as regards their disappointment and lateness in their fulfillment and target.

Being at alert to make a contribution or impact in life is what directs your attention to a strict watching and waiting for the opening of the opportunity within your arm's length to exploit your worth to generate your desire.

A man needs to be desperate and eager in consistent manner to accomplish his projected vision, but his desperation must be guided and made legal to have his position attained. Life is all about trying till a mission is attained. A man should never look at his first attempt of what will yield what he wants. You are made more energetic and vibrant base on what you go through, which however means that, all that you attempt or go through in life are more important to your degree of achievement most times.

This chapter however is relating on what your position should be to get what you want. If possible you must be awaken all through with your eyes widely opened in the sense that, internally, you must be awaken and mentally set, you must not sleep, which means you must create an avenue for consistent thinking and forging ahead to accomplish when your motive is yet to be accomplished.

To cherish what you have, you must know the need of it, the value and how to put it into use. When what you have is known, understood and identified by you and you are utmost in applying it to reveal your intention, and to bring your motive to manifestation, the tendency of losing it and being void is drastically reduced, hence, the need to realize the reason why you must not lose what you have counted precious to make you.

CHAPTER FOUR (4)

APPRECIATE YOUR SKILL AND POTENTIAL

We are moving ahead as we study more of the need to cherish the available potential that can make men. This chapter is to point out the need for you as an individual to appreciate yourself first, if at all no one is there to appreciate you. There is no way man can appreciate your view at all times, there is no way there will not be discouragement or action that displeases your interest to reverse your position or pre-tangential opinion, but in all as regards the limitation and discouragement and distress that tend to exterminate you and your vision, you must be the subject pillar and corner stone of your vision to make it real.

Just like the attitude of the people that are celebrated as successful today, when they fall, they appreciate themselves and put in more of the effort to do greater things other than what fell them. A man should stand at the gap of encouraging himself if at all no one is there to appreciate his dexterity. When one knows how to appreciate himself and he believes in what he has, and not discouraged of his focus, then, he has all what it takes to be a champion and to excel.

When a man calls himself a mechanical engineer, he should be able to do all things in relation with the mechanical fault in a vehicle. But I have seen an individual naming himself carburetor master, instead of his area of specialization on the kind of the series of products, e.g, Toyota, Honda, Peugeot etc.

This man must have really identified and understood better of a certain thing or the other which have made him to be concentrated on the specific operation. And desirably, he must have had the interest in what he does to appreciate his specific angle of his distinctive unique performance that can add value to his skill and potential. Though every other mechanic can do what he does, and very possible, they claim to know it better than him, but people still patronize him base on the name and the appreciation of his personal worth and value.

Also, I found it very discomforting and funny in the attitude of the most of the West African countries, who find it extremely difficult to appreciate their team at their home country, but appreciate the clubs outside the context of their countries, while they expect the best from them when they are engaged in the international matches and so forth. Without a doubt, the performances will automatically be depressive because the sense of the appreciation of the worth and value of the team has never been in place prior to their engagement in such a competition. What I am trying to make a clarification on should not be left out without catching up with it to make it a very relevant measure for an upgrade. Appreciation of your skill and potential is very relevant to make up the visibility of what your intention looks like.

A Nation that does not appreciate what she has will definitely be a nation of no importance and might not be able to arrive at her conclusive end or destination. When what you have is not appreciated, someone else who knows better of what you have will definitely make use of that which you have not appreciated to bring out the best to make his purpose and objective a reality and awesome.

In most of the West African countries, quite disappointing that we are most at times never in support of our citizens, and that has resolved to the issue of brain drift which had made most of the population of the adequate mind to migrate to other part of the world where there is more worth to life. We have recorded thousands of disused men that are of the best worth and intellect in term of creativity, innovation and their contribution in the aspect of their dexterity.

Sometimes, someone with a million of naira or other currency might find it very difficult to know the importance and the advantages he has over others, by his lavish spending , probably because of not working for the money or having no difficulty prior to having the right and privilege to such financial capability, whereas, we have thousands of other individuals that pray for only 10,000 of whatever currency to start up their businesses which however at the long run might be so giant to even finance the man that is termed to be a millionaire at a period in time.

The issue is that, as soon as you discover yourself, you must be able to appreciate what you have, else you will lose it to the hand of another man that knows better of its value and usefulness. Appreciating your skill makes you to understand that your worth remains your worth under all forms of circumstances, to prove and to demonstrate that which is inbuilt in you without any form of inferiority or looking down on that which is your personal gift.

When you appreciate your skill, you will surely know the reason why you must put it to use and to understand the reason why you have it. Just as said earlier, there is nothing in this life you possess that you have not put into use that can bring forth any positive result. You must be able to start up a particular activity to have an end of your expectation. Though not all action you embark on that yields the result of expectation, but there is no action you have engaged with that will not reveal a new scope and idea when it is well analyzed and adequately given an ideal attention.

I have encountered many individuals without arms and limbs carrying out a function or the other in life just because of the appreciation of the themselves and what they possesses in them, believing that if only for that, they are not a waste and must under must make their impact through the grace of life they have been endowed.

When you have an appreciation on what you have, this will automatically pave way into how it can be put to use and make you to accomplish purpose, hence, what you have will be your desire at all cost to make you.

CHAPTER FIVE (5)

VALUE DEVELOPMENT AND UPGRADING

There is necessary importance to examine what development and upgrading mean before the real sense of the message can be meaningful to the reader.

What is upgrade or upgrading? This is an act of having an improvement in an operation standard, value or method to meet with the existing and prevailing condition and circumstance at hand. This is a way at which a standard is fortified or improved on to yield a better result other than its present value. It connotes brightness in the philosophy of the world as regards the improvised manner of adding more meaningful advantages to the result at hand.

When one thinks of development, this is a growth that it is visible in all aspects of the operation that makes a whole. This is an avenue of having a perfect effect and positive impartation on all aspect of functionality which however is feasible in the total evaluation and standardization of one's intention and impression. It is an upgrade that has to do with the entire life of one's potential and traits to fit-in into the circumstance at hand and thinking of its suitability for the futuristic purpose.

However, value development and upgrading is very important to have access to opportunity, varieties of option to flourish as human.

And sincerely, this is a must for all to do from time to time in order to make oneself very relevant and not only that, but to be fixed up and to be involved in the changes in the world in holistic.

Development, upgrading or learning are terms that are quite synonymous in the sense that, they both point at the same direction while looking at adding value to human and organization. And just as said, very pivot for all human to work on it to have the genuineness of purpose and diverse options to move and to blend up with the storm of the world.

This important aspect of life can however be witnessed in different manner and stylish way. And these are as follows:

(1)   Education/Academic: this is an improvement that is sometimes back up with certificate and sometimes uncertificated. This is the advance way of formal western language and level of expanding the knowledge and bringing about newness and innovation in the environment and the world at large. It is a place at which brightness is given to the life of men to bring about the imaginary things to real life situation, where impossibility is made to be understood to be possibility through various theories, testing, writing and verbal communication with the proof of the various result that had been recorded at every point in time.

Though sometimes, it is very difficult to proof its usefulness in relation to the series of subjects that one pass through while growing, but either directly or indirectly, it has its mighty impartation in the degree of its importance in the life of whosoever that has been made through this channel. It gives a sense of belongingness and makes a psychological and mental balance in the sense that anyone who is advantaged of it, believes in his worth and value, though not all that are yet to be made; because of the intellectual quotient that is vastly important to be in operative to make a meaningful creation out of the exposure.

(2)   **Vocational studies:** this can be said to be an avenue at which skill and

potential can be perfectly exhibited. This is when one is made to either go through training in line with his choice of interest or being control to have something doing to have a competitive life and at the same time to have a good standard of living. Unlike in academics, in which what you do sometimes does not correlate with what you see outside the citadel of learning, that is, activities that most at times fill with theories which can be propounded on the air but never come to manifestation, vocational learning takes one through the very practical aspect of what a man intends to be. And sincerely, at each point in time, a man can easily identify himself in relation to what his worth and value looks like. Candid, this form of learning is made very compulsory in some of the advanced and developed countries, this has in one way or the other assisted tremendously in what many nation have become, whereas, in the developing nation our interest is more concentrated on how sophisticated our certificate looks like even without any form of its injection into the economics of the world or expansion in the existing border of the intellectual effort.

(3)   Self-initiation and idea/learning: this is the cheapest way of learning most especially in an environment that is too harsh or unfriendly to the citizen of her country. This is a situation in which individuals tend to look into what they can generate with what they have through their initiative and inbuilt composition and intellectual power. In same view, we have some plant growing naturally, outbreak of diseases springing up without knowing the causes, disaster happening without any cause e t c. We have some individuals that come up without any formal or informal education to make a new life and doing what is quite important to living than what the highest scholars have been able to detect or working on. Though each individual possess this form of unique greatness of honour of a specific function to create a new beginning for an action, but not all can withstand the rigor and challenges. Therefore, this is a way at which without any lesson or teaches of any kind, people struggle to make their way into the system of a perfect living. This should have been the best of all the avenues of getting knowledge, but sometime might be very vigorous and cumbersome to have a break through. Also most at times, people do the wrong things in the right way and vice versa without any one to counsel or instruct them, which eventually leads to waste of time, resources and man power.

(4)   Reading text books and other educational books: this is an avenue at which people acquire information that can lead to their improvement in the various types of journals, articles, text books and other series of educational books. The book reading is part of the books under discussion. Without being in the class room or having any informal related acquisition of knowledge, one may still get information through reading, provided he can read to understand the content of the books he reads.

(5)   Listening to information: another aspect which is worth to be mentioned is the issue of listening to information. Most people are yet to be able to have a succeeding outcome just because they are not able to generate the adequate information that should allow them to know when and on what to apply what they have. Having access to information is never only done by the series of the enlisted point mentioned, but can as well be extracted through the necessary information of all kinds that one might be exposed to while moving ahead. When you have the access to the due information, you have access to what it takes to be where to be. The value of information a man is advantaged of translates to his real value to make his intention worthwhile. Through information, there is always an upgrade and notification of what is in existence that can take the foresight of a man to the stage of excellence and full manifestation. This can however be tapped into through listening and making findings that are lucrative to the nature of the development in perspective of the whole lots of the ideas that one is aiming to accomplish or attain.

(6)   Observation and attention: it is very important to know that observation and attention towards the varieties of the activities around oneself are very compulsory to have a huge translation to the realm of expectation. One must be very familiar with his environment and the things that are revolving around within it. There must be an evaluation of the result of the occurrences around you to determine the sets of ideas and operations that should enhance you the fortress to the advancement and to decline. If care is not taken, and one is not too observant, what had lead someone to a state of know where might be the very line of your focus in the same manner that such an action has been undertaken. In most of the African countries, imitating of another person's ideas and business acumen is more rampant. I am not condemning the act out rightly, but my position is that, if at all you need to be involved in such an action leading to using

of another person's view, it must be well
assessed and you must be very sure of the
ending thereof. Being observant and
giving attention to the activities around
are however the tool to have a conclusive
result of the economic benefit of these
set of existing operations and activities.
Therefore, one may look into the aspect
of observation and attention while
looking into the personal upgrade and
development.

In all the different options enlisted, they
are all embedded with the advantages
and disadvantages, but in all, one must be
able to learn, to gain better on the
prevailing activities and to be able to be
at alert for the changes that arises in the

future.

However, value development and upgrading are very essential and important to be able to do exploit and not only that, but to get to the stage of full realization of human potential and worth.

When you develop or upgrade yourself, it means you cherish what you have, and this however interpret to you the reason why it must never be wasted or be allowed to be lost.

CHAPTER SIX (6)

DO NOT DESPISE YOUR SKILL AND TALENT

One of the most rampant of the behavioral system of the human is the attitude of despising their skill and potential most especially when such skill is yet to be productive and active or to be beneficial to their immediate want, desire and their environment. Your skill and talent might take you years before it is matured to be appreciated, and sincerely, it takes processing to develop yourself to the level of general acceptance or full recognition.

What you start up that many count no meaning to, must without any doubt sometimes, someday be appreciated if it is given the very best of all effort to make it a reality and worthwhile. A mango tree planted can never yield its result or expected fruit without a constant nurture and giving it a space to mature to the stage of yielding its fruit.

A man must not despise what he has at the very beginning of its existence to have a result of the true worth of his life's composition. What you can do and what you have as an inbuilt on innate ability or acquired and you are well grounded on can never be measured in monetary parlance or indeed questionable in its worth. You must be friendly and of cordial relationship with your skill and talent, and be focused on how it can be put into use rather than looking out for an easy alternative which deflates the genuine work nature of a man.

When a man fails to despise his skill and potential, these elements of honour and growth will definitely force him to be elevated to the level of his dream and desire to be completely made. A talent and skill not wasted or despised is a talent that makes the real intention of a man to come true and into manifestation. And it is a must to jealously guide and cherish such a predicated gift of God to be able to place them adequately as their needs arise.

If you are a talented footballer, that everybody recognizes and give the due respect on the football pitch whenever you are in the team playing, and suddenly because of an option that does not guarantee your continuity, but can give you more financial power temporarily, you opt out. Though, the very immediate benefit of such option might raise up for the time being, but might not be able to withhold you for a long time. Also, since your ambition is rested on the financial viability of the particular option, you might not be able to duely analyze the thorough details that its continuity entails, which might eject such an individual out of such a track within a short time period. What you have as innate ability is quite very essential compares with what you try to learn to be able to accomplish. In the very first instance, there is every tendency to grow and glow without no limit, whereas, the second decision might lead to a sudden stoppage or return one back to the initial stage.

Most of the so called successful business man in the world are in the bracket of those who have not despise what they have as their composition. However, to be where you have planned to be, and to be destined and reclaim your possession, you must be very careful and conscious of how your values are injected into the system around you, to make you, else, you will never stop complaining and grumbling despite the fact that you are well position and well paid, but reverse is the case of being friendly with yourself or worth.

If you are still one of those who believe in destiny charger or approves that someone can change your destiny, I want to implore you today with the encounter you have with this book, that if truly that which you have seen and known how to do best is what you do in a unique manner, to attract and catch the attention of the populace, you will surely without a single doubt flourish, and you will be able to testify to my conclusive argument, that a man is unstoppable when he knows better of his bearing and he gives all what it takes him to be there.

Conclusively, when you cherish your value and talent, you will without doubt understand better of the need not to despise it, to make it a contributory element to your growth and development, and not only that, but to have a special impartation in the existence. This will however make you to have the passion and zeal never to allow your talent and skill to be wasted or lost.

CHAPTER SEVEN (7)

DO NOT ACCEDE WITH RELEGATION, BUT BE RELEVANT

What constitutes relegation is never how people treat you or how acceptable or reject able you are, but your un-willingness and inactive role in making yourself relevant and being who you are out-rightly.

A man must be so active to the tune of making himself available and prepared to live a symbolic life that can affect his environment positively.

When one says relegation, this means an act of making or placing human in a second cadre or level of living and operation. This is when a man is made not to be functional as regard a reason or the other for the benefit of another man or himself to make a contribution. This can be termed to be state at which another man pronounces a state of inferiority on another man which however affects his status and his level of operation physiologically and in his performance. It is a state of saying that, someone is not part and parcel of the first class group of individual or group of people which however directly or indirectly refers him to operate at the states of mediocrity.

On the other hand, when one checks the word relevance, this simply means the significance and the premier state and stage of a man or something in the evaluation states. Relevance does not mean that something is the most pivot or premier, but this is only saying that, something is very crucial in value when examined. It is stating and showing the importance of a part in the whole structure or composition. This is to say that, something is so essential that, when it is dealt without in a particular scenario, it has a degree of magnitude of distortion and impairment which could have added a special taste and specific worth to the issue of discourse.

This chapter is only trying to give courage to the less courageous and people who easily get intimidated as a result of the pressure they witness or encounter in one way or the other while trying to exhibit their worth of talent and idea. Though, the pressure rules around you, as a man, you must know that distraction is never an impediment to be known or counted important when aiming at being relevant. Whatever the issues you cut across in life, there must be a sense of ownership of what you have to be able to stand on your position to defend what you have to attain.

Yes, indeed, there are thousands of people that are self-motivated and can create opportunity for themselves without any one instructing them, but that has nothing to do on your own worth of value and what can be created through you when you are well set for making impact if at all you can not create one but willing to make the maximum exploitation of things in existence.

The moment a man stands to be defeated of the invisible challenges which are meant to be the encouraging factor to him, he stands to experience the disconnection between himself and what he can achieve or make to come to reality. However, the need for the previous chapter to be understood to understand the essence of what a man has, to be able to stand at all times to defend it irrespective of what another possess or the prevailing circumstances around him.

The usual saying says, no one can make you inferior without your own consent. Really, this is what this particular chapter is saying. You must never count yourself inferior in life with whatever any one does or says, but must be challenged to do more. There are thousands of things you can do, and several approaches of arriving at the stated goal that is differentiated from that of every other one, which when you discipline yourself on and capitalized on, make you a distinct entity and great achiever.

The point remains that, an experience not shared is an experience not necessary, because what you can see that others cannot see or feel is like a dream not shared. And this will never add a single value to you or the environment you live. However, the need to exhibit your nature and your experiences to make a life and create a unique different view and idea that others will be forced to imbibe after a testing of its appropriateness and acceptance.

Though it seems what you have is not enough, but mind you, what you have is quite more essential and worthwhile than what many have, which simply reveals the interest of the others in that which you have that they do not have.

You are extremely relevant in the context of things that emanates around your environment and within any space or association you have found yourself. It is a must to make a contribution of that which you know, to be able to have a test of it and to challenge the already existing hypothesis.

I was on my daily job sometimes, and that faithful day, there was a heavy down pour which made all terrain of the land to be flooded and water lodged. Surprisingly, the public transport in which I was stopped or entrapped in, between a very widen and deepen pothole on the road that was made up of flood thereafter brought about the issue of how to make a way down to a dry place.

Suddenly, a man came around and volunteered himself to lift people one after the other at an exorbitant amount, to my surprise, all of us in the bus of about 60 passengers acceded and with a very serious combat queue up, for this unexpected assistant which was very crucial at this point in time. What I am trying to deduce out of this is that, if this man had made himself not relevant, no one could or would have reckon with his relevance.

Though, he was one of the so called not useful and the touts, but at this particular place and situation, he was made to be the saviour of lives in which I was involved as a result of not wanting to have stain on my gorgeous dressing and pair of shoes.

A man must never for once look down on himself to the level that he is no more relevant in a place he is. A disadvantage on your part in a way or the other should give you a better advantage to be where you should be. What makes someone to be against of what you know and can do sometimes is as a result of his limitation in the degree of his intellectual power to evaluate you completely, which should ordinarily makes you another man that can operate at a higher stage and pedestrian higher than your discourager when you move ahead to add up the necessary values that can distinctively analyze your intention to such an individual and the whole lots of the others.

We are still looking at cherish what you have not to lose it, and in other to have a comprehensive thought and consideration, we are looking at never let anyone relegate you or make you irrelevant. What you can do or be in life is as a result of what you have in you if only you are the architect of your life, not otherwise a wagon. There is however the need to press forward and further to realize yourself when no one can find you, and at all cost to try to make your value important in all circumstances, and not on that alone, but make your presence extremely relevant to the level of breaking the scope of barrier of any hindrance and obstacle on your pathway to success.

CHAPTER EIGHT (8)

PROOF YOUR CONCEIVABLE IDEAS BEYOND DOUBT TO MATERIALIZE

This chapter is to relate on what it takes a man to have a completeness and fulfillment in life. An idea or dream that cannot be proved beyond the mere need of it might not really make any important value in the life of men or in their heart. Do not forget that we have numerous men that are thinkers, therefore, you must be able to have an empirical theories that can be demonstrated prior to it being accepted. There is need to understand perfectly what your mind is trying to reflect, and not only that, to know the reason why a detailed analysis should be given to it for its materialization.

Inability to proof what you have correlates with the topic just treated in the previous chapters. There is need to have all what it takes to give the real meaning of what you have to share. Nothing good in life comes easily, so also, something that is bad. What I am saying is that, for people to have the due believe in what you have or the new notion or vision you are trying to bring forth, you must be able to proof this thought beyond the ordinary. You must be very up and doing to compete with the rigor and challenges of it, which expands your acumen of understanding on such a project better and explain the reason why you must make it above the degree of limitation in its existence.

We have thousands of theories propounded by various theorists which have been concurred with and accepted by the world at large. This was due to the ability and interest to make it well known to the entire world. It must never have been too easy to make it up to the state of acceptance and of great value and benefit to the development, if not for the unending commitment to make it such it is. To have an idea to sell to the world, there must be a priority of given the very best of your effort to proof it beyond doubt. This is what gives the conviction of its viability and attractiveness to the populace, to have it as option and to accept it after series of testing.

If your intention is not proven, you might not be too courageous to defend what you have. This simply means that, this must have come to being either by chance or coincidence which means you might not be able to repeat the theory when there is quest to have it.

If your idea or notion or view is not developed to the level of materialization, it amounts to what I can term to be waste of time, resources, and humanity. I often consider the man that developed the initiative of making electric bulb; it took him several attempts and years before he could come forth to the stage of stabilization. After several attempts, if the man was un-able to come forth to the stage of its success and reality, it would have been a disgrace, though not when you look at it in an advanced level. Also, it would have been turned to wastage in resources and life span without a symbolic accomplishment.

The history reveals that, the man had never been to any school, and he has never gone through any training to bring this into actualization, but what he could see had indulged and energized him to get to the conclusive region that its glory still radiates till now. I think there is no household that does not use bulb in their houses at this dispensation of civilization, and if yet, we have people that are yet to start up to use it, they will without any doubt get to know of its essentiality sometimes and someday.

A housewife that says she can cook better than that of your mother should be able to experiment and proof it to you. Not ordinarily by saying sake you should believe in that. There is virtually nothing that you can say you know how to do that does not have a particular way of proving it. So, you should be very set in all to make your intention proven to the state of conviction of whosoever that has not believe in it, to accept it in either voluntary or in-voluntary way.

We are still looking at cherish what you have not to lose it and candid, if what you possess is not cherished, there can never be an impression to proof your intention to the acceptable level, so also, there might not be any need to work on it till it becomes realized in life. All what you are and can be can however be proved through your action to make the entire world to have controversy on your standard and thereafter reckon with the empirical philosophical exhibition.

CHAPTER NINE (9)

INVEST TIME ON WHAT YOU HAVE PASSION TO DO.

What is an investment? This is an act of doing a certain thing that has a positive contribution to the resources of tomorrow or the time to come. It is a futuristic planning ahead for a better nature of expansion and more pleasing and pleasant time period. It is a strategy of working what you have to work out what to have. It is a projection of using little to create a bigger dream and comfort in the nearest future for the desire or anticipation. It can simply be referred to as suffering or going through a certain condition for a better condition in the time to come. It is self-denial for self-enjoyment. This is when what you are is

less to give the meaning of what your expectation looks like. It is a thing of interest or choice to have a better chance of the controlling power of the future events. It is an avenue of creating and making provision for the time that the prevailing provisions might not exist any more. It is an act of using what you have to get what you want.

However, the motive of investment is to have a future on the investment. Returns on the investments are what the investment yields while the investment remains static. It is the product of investment. It can be said to be the result that comes out of what you have labored for. This is what the investment creates at the point of its maturity to the owner of the investment. One can look at it as the proceeds from the investment.

At the point at which the investment yields its returns, the return does not impair or negatively affect the investment or its functionality. Candid speaking, without adding up to what you have invested, if the due depreciation calculation is imbibed or when it is a stock market or other economic related functions, the investment keeps growing bigger without any other contribution at the pace and space of favourable economic stability and absence of inflation of the price power.

I am only trying to pass across the intention behind the sub topic "invest time on what you have passion for". When a man discovers what his talent or skills look like, there is an utmost need to give better margin of time to it, to make it worthwhile to live. What you invest on is what make you and not only that, this is what provides you various signal to different direction at which you are supposed to function. A man must invest on something to get through huddles and the challenges of life when they come. Things such as Academics, Talents building, Vocational training, Personal development etc are what comprise investment that is expected of a man to be able to reach out to his descriptive situation and focus.

Without investing your life on anything spectacular and worthwhile, you may stand to gain nothing in life. No one was made or created to be wasted, but mostly, all who find it difficult to have a placement often tends to miss out of investing their time on a profitable and lucrative thing that can make them.

Sometimes, one may work and give the very best and yet no result, but if there is hope on what you have invested on, if at all the pain waxes stronger, there will be a great assurance that the pain can only stand for a while, whereas, the remedy must without no doubt be given. There is need to have something substantial to save or invest time on, but quite pathetic, most often, people waste time on things that might not add up to what makes them up.

So annoying that people give their precision and precious time and inestimable priceless value to the development of the others for years before making up their mind to resolve and tackle the existing fear of the unknown that ties them down. Without seeing the reason to be relevant in life, one might find it very complex to make it to the stage at which he is meant to function efficiently and effectively.

You must give at all times your focus and attention to what you have perceived that can give you an advantage ahead of every other ones. It takes you deep thought to realize yourself. It takes you a quick notice of what astonishes people to make your way in. It takes courage to stand to invest in your ambition to be made. It takes you investing on what you cherish and that you have the conviction on, to be an exceptional being. You must be separated before a due separation that brings honour to you in your endeavors. In relation to investment, this serves as the talent, skill, acquired knowledge or resources that are made to make a man. And what I am trying to say is that, each man must find a time out of no time to spend time on the things which will definitely make them a giant in the time to come. Each individual is an architect of his life, and sincerely, anyone that fails to plan might have nothing to reap. A life must attract a purpose that can yield result and makes ideology to be well known by the world. When you are known for what you are, and what you are is essential to living, you will be made base on what you are and sincerely, that differentiation will definitely pronounce your value and appropriately give you the right value in the midst of the others.

Mostly, while committing oneself on a better disposition and standard that can change ones situation, the journey looks so untidy and un-lucrative, but the submission and the endurance bring out the special features of what you have and the limit at which you can go. The journey that leads to the bright destination is at the initial stage not very pellucid and sometimes gloomy, but the end of it gives the very best definition that makes it up. For example, the initiation of the air craft was mocked till the very moment at which the aircraft flew, and till today, though he was not a scholar, but both the learned and the unlearned make use of his initiative and contribution to the world at large. So also the man that came up with the idea of the system (computer software), he affirmed, that there will be a time that everyone will be connected with the aid of various soft wares irrespective of their location or place of abode, but he was greatly mocked and people disagreed to agree though he was never a scholar.

Your view is very relevant when you can give your time and yourself to understanding it, and not only that, but to experiment it and look at how its economic benefit can surface.

Give your time often to that which you understand and know that you have passion to do; this will definitely make you an exceptional being when you are adequately made. Out of no time that you eat and catch fun with the others irrelevantly, make out a special interest to invest at all cost your time most especially on what can make you and permit you to stand not at the presence of the mere men.

Let all your resources be made available for that which can set you apart and create new person of honour of your desire and dream. You must count your resources only significant when they can avail you of the opportunity to address the issue of your life and talent building, and all what you have to make you.

A man must look around to get more knowledge. Getting more knowledge that can add up value to you and your potential is also one of the greatest investment that a man can have. You must look around and struggle at all cost to build yourself up around that which you possess. The knowledge however tells you what next as the talent and skill to be used are already available in you.

Being friendly with your view and passion makes you to cherish it more and to be more involved in being engaged with it from time to time till something spectacular and meaningful comes out of it. Being friendly has to do with how often you make use of your time and skill when there is an advantage to doing so. However, it is a must to be friendly with what you have to make a success of it.

There are thousands of things which must be considered and properly put in place to be able to have a good ending or result of investment in life. Let us consider this point and thereafter move ahead to another chapter, this is learning of something unique and new in the processing and the activities that brings up or builds your talent. You must be very simple hearted and humble to learn on your processing of being made. Life itself is the greatest teacher that explains the circumstances revolving around it in a clearer manner than how any other one can do. When you are so calm and humble minded to learn out of what you do, there is every tendency of never fallen a victim of failure of such circumstances that mislead human any more in life if you can have a success your mission and focus. Also, there is an advantage ahead of every other ones who have not tried or know about the subject matter of making provision for attempt and trial of their genuinely innate capacitation. What you have learnt will definitely strike your heart on how a better nature of your effort can be made to attune to the issues and the condition existing at a particular time.

Conclusively, investing your time on what you have passion for has brought us to this extent of looking at the benefit of investing one's time to gain excessively of the futuristic pre intention of one's desire and purpose. When a man fails to invest, he does not cherish what he has, and when you fail to cherish, the worth and the value of what you have is never understood which makes one extremely careless of evaluating and securing that which he has till it is lost. However, man must under must cherish that which he has and build on it strongly not to lose it.

CHAPTER TEN (10)

GUARD AND PRESERVE WITH INTEGRITY THAT WHICH YOU HAVE

The term integrity really matters and plays an important role in getting to a full realization of what a man proposes to do. Without an integrity there will be wide gap and margin in becoming what you are ordinarily meant to be, because the past relationship with others sometimes depict who exactly you are, and what you may do or not.

Integrity however means willingness not to compromise with the dirty and dusty nature of the activities of the world. This is being part of the world and not of the worldly. It can simply be said to be of the honesty and straightforwardness to make an intention a reality. This means due consideration of the others ahead of yourself. Thinking on how not to go beyond the set boundaries and gaps that separate the right of someone else from that of yours. It can be said to be un-condemnable facts and reality. Integrity is self-control from the selfishness, most especially when a little or larger resource is given as at the time you are not directly under the control or supervisor of another higher authority.

Integrity means the attitude that makes you to understand the vanity in the worth of the material substances in life entirely. It is a source of looking ahead to the future and life after death to have a substantial contribution which the upcoming or those who read through your legacy and way of life finds interesting and worthy of emulating to have a better natured standard.

However, the need by each an individual to take into consideration how to cherish, guard and preserve the value and worth they have not to lose them. What a man had done and suffered to get for years in life can easily be misplaced or destroyed within a second.

Reputation is a difficult thing to manage when you are yet to understand the need to have it, but very easy to build and maintain if you have decided to be a champion and a free man indeed. It is one of the fastest things that can be tarnished. It takes years to arrive at what your intention looks like or to be made, but it takes a single minute to have a total destruction and devaluation of worth and integrity if care is not taken.

After a man had understood what his composition looks like, there is always the need to continuously nurture and to work on how the value under examination can be made more adequate and vibrant. Whenever you stop doing what you like to do for a day or more, it tends to path you in a double paste. What I meant is that if you leaves what you do for a day, such a thing leaves you for 2days. There is need to have a passion and a continuous investment to what you have passion on to be able to do it in a better manner.

One of the related ways to guide and preserve your value is the ability to work yourself separated from the crowd. Separating yourself away from the crowed does not mean that you should not associate with others, but you must be able to do things or carry out activities in a different conversion to make common sense out of the uncommon at the time of its performance. This is the situation at which circumstances is converted to its best. It can be said to be using the time that people or majority are confused or dismayed to create a solution to their challenges.

In another language, one can also be talking of timeliness and giving oneself all through to the projected duration of an agreed functionality. This still form the part of the integrity that I referred to and discussed, there must be control on the level of commitment and proposal not to make an empty agreement; any conclusive intention must be carried out at the duration of the scope of the projected plan. Many company and individuals have lost their glory as a result of being unable to meet the standard of their promises or the position they stand on. Time resources is quite very essential to be noted and clearly previewed to meet up with a task ahead and thereafter have an integrity in any commitment. There must be projection and looking ahead to make a particular project accomplished, under no circumstance should you as a corporate or individual gives a timeframe that cannot give a result to a client. When you are defined with your way of delivering, and accomplishing, without failure or disappointment, you will have no option than having a better advantage on the others as regards how you will be patronized.

Say with a simple language of those things that you can accomplish and do or that you know how to do, other than promising heaven and earth on the things that you can not do or on which you might find difficult to do. Many at times, most of us rush into a conclusion probably because of what we have discovered to gain, other than the actual mission and purpose to act on. And candid, if at all, one or two individual have been misled, the others might be more-wiser to be preventive and cautious of falling a victims probably because of the information extracted on the record at hand or your historical antecedent.

What are mine saying? As an individual, you must be very set to know that, it is a must to guide and preserve with integrity that which you have not to lose it. If what you have is not cherished, there can never be any need to guide it or preserve it with integrity because then, it means that you have not placed the adequate value or the purported evaluation on it, which invariable means that the need to cherished it might not be required. Integrity is what can make a man to be adequately represented when he is not present, it generate goodwill and cleared representation that the world prefer to build on even without direct contact than someone well known but of disrepute character.

Integrity has nothing to do with your gain and procedure of attaining your motive, but it is of more concern to the nature of promises and the capability to deliver without placing anyone who is in agreement with you to undue anxiety and long expectation or frustration and fraud. One of the virtues that must never be toyed with, that we have taken with levity in the most African nations is integrity.

Most of the younger ones do not even care for their integrity to be wasted at the detriment of having riches, and the elderly ones that should be good example to the growing ones are mostly found uncontrollable in the midst of managing the resources and physical funds.

There is need to make it known to the world in whole that, integrity is far more valuable compares with any form of the worth of money or fund that might be acquired, and with this, we must be fine-tuned on how best this can be succinctly glorified in our societies. When a good integrity is created for the future use, there will be a standard provision for the future erection of purpose and accomplishment of greater desire. This is because good works are never easy to be forgotten. However, the need to cherish what you have to be rightfully connected, create a future of purpose and not to lose it for something that is not glorified.

CHAPTER ELEVEN (11)

SELL YOUR PRODUCT AND SERVICES, NOT YOUR IDEAS.

What do I mean by this statement? There is wide difference between your idea and what you can produce with your idea.

When one refers to product, it means the very outcome of one's idea, that is, what the combination of various components of a man can make with the different kind of resources available to make it. Product is an act of coming forth with a specific result that is planned to create the business development initiative. It is the generation or creation of any particular thing in an aligned manner with the view of the foresight a producer to accomplish a plan in association with the economic benefit of such an establishment, or an act of multiplying to get a certain figure that will be necessary to have a genuine contribution to the activities around the world. In the formal self-definition, one will clearly extract that, something must be mixed or multiply with another thing to make it a whole or to have a produce.

Whereas, ideas means, what a man can conceive within him, his notion, thought and consideration. It can as well be described to be an intellectual power to have a deep thought on what comes up within either afresh or imitating the already existing production to have an upgrade. It can be said to be a mental impression of a certain event or planning for a purpose in the mind.

However, the deduction in the statement is that, it is better to sell your product than selling what you have as an idea. Idea in worth is never quantifiable and estimable in the sense that, having an idea means that, you have priceless information, because it is never practiced or evaluated. Factually, there is no issue or circumstance that is in operation or existence that were not in a time or the other conceived before they were made. Most of these activities were not evaluated appropriately before they materialized, while the ones that were clearly studied and out rightly comprehended on marks the prestigious ones that are celebrated and excel.

Many mostly believe in the best they can get as a result of venturing into a particular action or the other, but most at times, what the feed-back looks like is quite differentiated compared to what they aim at. The impression I am trying to create is that, human ideas and thought are vast to the level that, at the point of their consideration or viewing them in their minds, the value and worth they can actually generate are not ascertained or accurate.

This however makes it very prudent and essential for a man to understand that idea is never such a thing that can be priced. Better it is, to have such ideas converted to their end means, products and services, before they are sold or consumed. The moment a particular commodity is produced, the value of it can be examined and as a result of this, the price can be evaluated, which can be favourable or otherwise in their evaluation.

Take for an example, the production of handset and computer. When the initiator conceived the ideas, they could never have ascertained the full potential of its use and cost, but rather, they knew that such commodities are essential to humanity for easy and better living. Though there is never any invention that can make a better living that will not sell, but what of if the invention was rejected and no one reckon with it, they might not have an edge way. Before those intentions, people were living and using the al-cake means, people communicate and perform virtually things that system or hand set can do, but in an olden manner that takes more than necessary period of time of having an expected result. These ideas were welcome as a result of ease and freedom that they injected into living.

However if all these kind of ideas were sold before they materialized, the glory would have been apportioned to another man, and not only the glory, but all the economic benefit and any other consideration to the pedigree of bringing up such an invention could have been lost.

Do not forget so soon that, the initiator of the Cola-cola caught up with the vision and discovered that it could make giant revenue to him if it is sold off rather than acting on it. But he made the decision to sell the initiative off to another man who foresaw the benefit of venturing into such idea. The point is this, the originator of the intention is far forgone, but Coca-cola is still in existence till today, and all the glory and celebration are apportioned to the owner of the organization and business.

In a nut shell, it is better for a man to react to his ideas as regards making them vivid and actualized before they are disposed or sell off. The value of idea is always very higher than any value you can give to the product you have in the sense that, it is only what you have physically that can be evaluated, not what you can conceive. Also, at the point of coming forth with what you have, there is every tendency of coming with something much greater and awesome than what you had at the inception of your thought. This means that, there is always a better privilege and amount of chances in your attempt to make a specific intention comes into manifestation. The more a man looks and implements his decision, the more he sees, and carries out an improvised standard that may take him to another capacity and realm entirely. Hence, there is need to give your time and yourself to making things happening

to see the need to cherish what you have
not to lose it.

CHAPTER TWELVE (12)

MAKE YOUR PRESENCE FELT AT ALL COST.

No one is expecting you to be greater than him in scope and value, but yet, in each a day, people tend to have growth and inspiration that is more worthwhile than what we have invoke or existence. A man should not continuously wait for his time without taking a radical decision to make himself available to be scheduled by the nature. Some people claim luck as regards their achievement, but I must sincerely tell you that, it is only a limited individual that can be lucky within this group of individuals before being made.

Your presence and what you have might not be noticed not until you commit yourself to it to make it known. You must consistently work towards your goal and vision till they come into manifestation. The available opportunities at which you can be known and recognized are so limited, and not only limited, but they are sometimes not attractive for you to fit into them. There is never anything that is not useful in life; such also is human in their composition. A man must fight and struggle greatly to be where he is meant to be if he wants to be there. (Studying outside the divine connection, divinely, all things are possible and can be accomplished without a single effort of physical interference).

It is never easy to have oneself separated or to be differentiated. Sometimes, it takes a man to decay completely before his season of flourishing comes and sometimes, it is just mere responding to the opportunity around that makes you a man. Your best must constantly be given to make your presence well felt in life. Without people feeling your presence, they might not know what value you have, and without knowing your value, they might not be able to position you where you should be.

Each man must have a specific drive moving them towards the actual direction at which they are made to be fulfilled. Expectation of a man however should not only be centered on those things that come to him freely but also, to those things that seems impossible to achieve. Most times, those things that are counted impossible are more convenient to arrive at, but looking at them from far off, they might not or never be accomplished because of the unnecessary attribute fictitiously ascribed to them.

Your decision matters in having what it entails you to live. Your reaction to events mostly stipulates what exactly you want in life. When a man is not eager or zealous to make a change, he might never see anything moving in his favour. Favour is just like a door and your ability and capacity is like the key to the door. The door might not be opened even when you possess the key without the attempt to open the door with the key. There must be an attempt to move forward to gain a better privilege to ascend to the predestined height and to rise to fame and prominence.

Most of the leaders we have recoded so far, though they were calm and sometimes very gentle, but at the point at which their intention is to be made known, the calmness disappears, while the form that reveals them with their intention is formulated towards their ambition.

If no one is giving you the avenue to be known, find all possible means to let out what you have to be displayed and exhibited. Let people see you with what you do, not saying what you do verbally.

Try to be involved in what you do to tell the world that what you know or can do is experiment able. There is never anything a man can come up with in life that will not attract criticism and rejection. But it is a must for you to be at alert to accommodate all forms of negativities till they are pronounced acceptable by the majority and eventually by the entire populace.

Many people forget soon, that what brings about placement, honour and contract is never who a man knows or his connection, do not get me wrong, sometimes, these are the yard sticks, but most at times, the ability and capability to courageously examine and exhibit what you have bring about fruitfulness and promotion.

I have experienced many individuals that believes that a certain thing or the other cannot be done by them, and yet, they turned out to be the best when it comes to testing them on the particular field. I have thousands of friends that believe that they cannot teach well, but the irony of it is that, whenever they teach, their students get the information better than that of the others who they think they could not compare themselves with.

Many have said that they do not know how to sing, and yet they turned out to be one of the fantastic singers that we can mention in life. What you consider you cannot do, are the things you can do when you put yourself into the action of having them accomplished. There must be thirst for the displaying of yourself at all times the opportunity is given, even though, what you think of is very hard and tasking. The set of complexities around are what can quickly make you known and let the society reckon with you when you can exhibit and attain them.

Try to make the impossibilities of life what can make you an avenue to arrive and to be known in the world. When you have a limited individuals that can make a provision for a certain result you can give, then you have better opportunity to get to the peak of your ambition and career. When others are saying no or thinking of I cannot, you must be able to say yes it is possible. Though it might not come as free as you can see, you can always arrive at where to be if prepared from within and you agree with your innate man to make it out.

Cherish that great product and inestimable value of your worth and composition not to lose it, do not be jealous about what other possess, but be proud of yourself and what you can do. Make an avenue to drive towards your vision at all times, and do not look at what other failed on as what you can fail on, but rather understand the separation and differentiation in you and the others in line with your level of performance and arriving at the conclusive end.

Be set at all times to give the very best of your potential. Do not value yourself as no body or second class individual or personality wherever you may find yourself, and be very set to admit constructive criticism rather than destructive ones that can cut you out of your vision. Be speedy to learn, most especially within your locality or environment, think on the things you can do to adapt to the changes that can elevate you when they are worked on.

CONCLUSION

Conclusively a man must cherish what he has not to lose it, and to display that you indeed cherish what you have, all aforementioned insight must be cross checked and worked on to make a step higher than ordinary which however brings about distinctiveness and uniqueness that catapults human to his destination. If what other possesses is what you cherish, then, you may never be satisfied or prepared to move ahead in life. But when you know that the little you have is enough to make you, then you tend to do mighty things with the little you have. No idea or contribution to life is little, but your contribution and what you have can be little when most especially you do not know how to place them or

when you have termed them to be little.
What you think is not valuable is what
many have used to excel and to have a
brighter future. You must give a
reasonable meaning to what you have,
you must give a deep thought on how
what you have can be impactful and
contributory to the whole existence, you
must think of the possibilities rather than
the impossibilities if truly you are aiming
at getting to the peak of the order of
making your worth relevant. Hence, the
need to cherish what you have not to lose
it might not attain its reality and its due
essence.

Good luck!!!

<u>CONTACT</u>

+234-803-718-4404   OR +234-808-093-5806

<u>tohyeva@yahoo.com</u>

TOPE ADENIJI, NIGERIA, WEST-AFRICA.

<u>SOLICITATION</u>

We solicit that the physical books should be requested from us for the use of the libraries, schools and the growing younger ones that might have one or two things extracted therein.

Also, we shall be glad to have your financial support for more production if your spirit directs.

Your constructive criticism can not be over emphasized.

Thank you.

www.ingramcontent.com/pod-product-compliance
Lightning Source LLC
Chambersburg PA
CBHW070128260726
48658CB00001B/315